Contents

New words

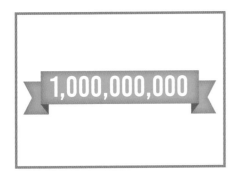

billion

blow away

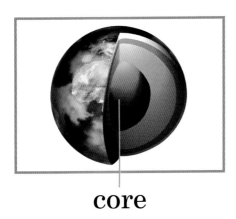

core

explosion

far

gas

group

grow

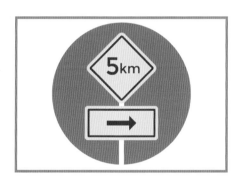

kilometre

size
(noun)

spacecraft

telescope

What is a star?

Look up at night.
What do you see?
You see lots of stars!
A star is very big and very hot.
It is a big ball of hot **gases**.

The Sun is a star!

star

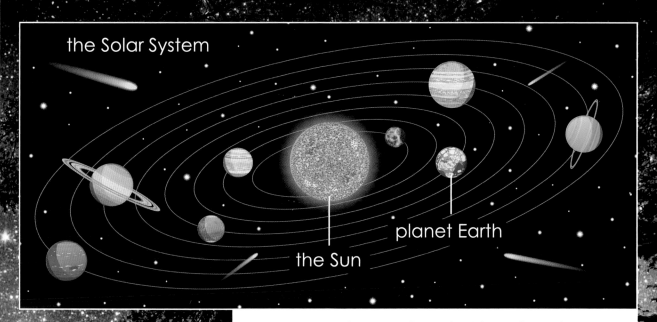

the Solar System

the Sun

planet Earth

Many stars have planets. The planets travel around the star. This is a solar system.

 **THINK!**

Is the Sun hot? How do you know?

Where do stars come from?

About 14 **billion** years in the past, there were no stars. Today, there are billions and billions of stars in space!

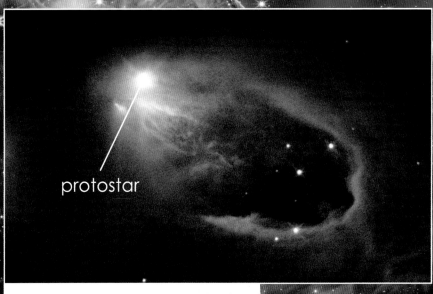

protostar

A protostar is a baby star.

Look at the nebula. A nebula is lots of gases. The gases come together and get very hot. Then the gases make a star.

space

nebula

▶ **WATCH!**

Watch the video (see page 32).
How old is Barnard's star? Is it older than the Sun?

Why are stars different colours?

All stars are hot, but a star's colour tells us how hot it is.

Stars are blue, white, yellow, orange or red.

Red stars are hot, but blue stars are very, very hot.

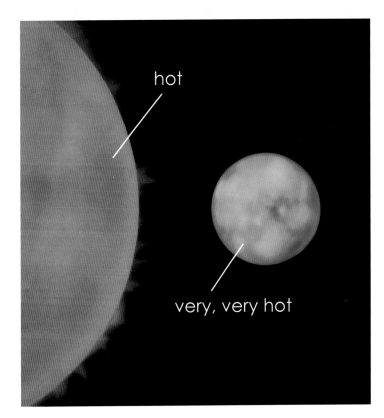

hot

very, very hot

The Sun is a yellow star.

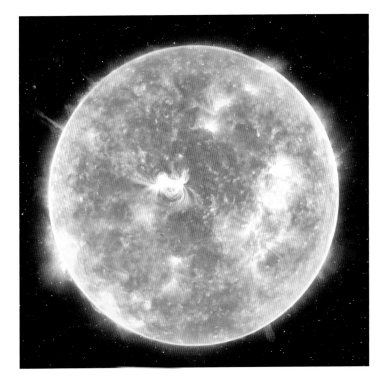

🔍 **LOOK!**

Look at the pages. What colours can stars be?

How big are stars?

dwarf star
(the Sun)

Earth

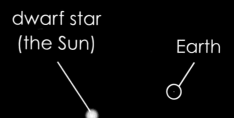

giant star

supergiant
star

All stars are big, but
they are different **sizes**.
Dwarf stars are small stars.
Hypergiant stars are very big stars.

hypergiant
star

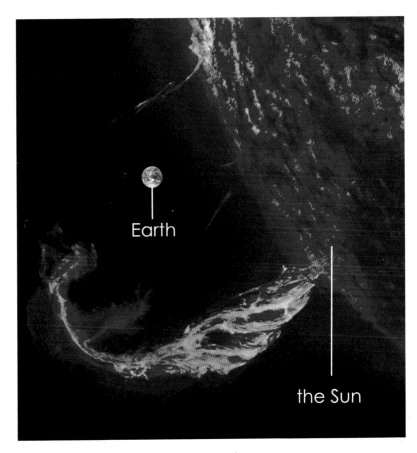

Earth

the Sun

The Sun is a yellow dwarf star.
It is a small star, but it is very big!

baby star

old star

The size of a star changes at different ages.

 **PROJECT**

Work with a friend. Make a poster about
Betelgeuse, a red supergiant star.

13

Can people travel to the Sun?

People cannot travel to the Sun because it is very hot. But we can send **spacecraft** there.

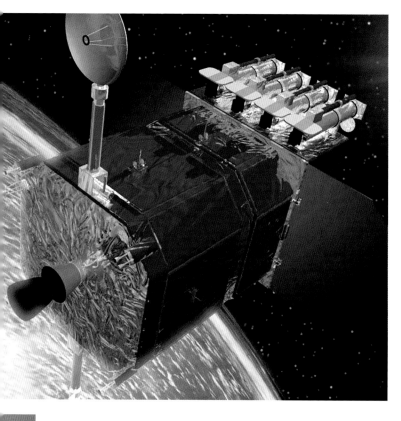

The Solar Dynamics Observatory helps us to understand the Sun.

In 2018, the Parker Solar Probe went to the Sun. This spacecraft can get very hot. It can get close to the Sun.

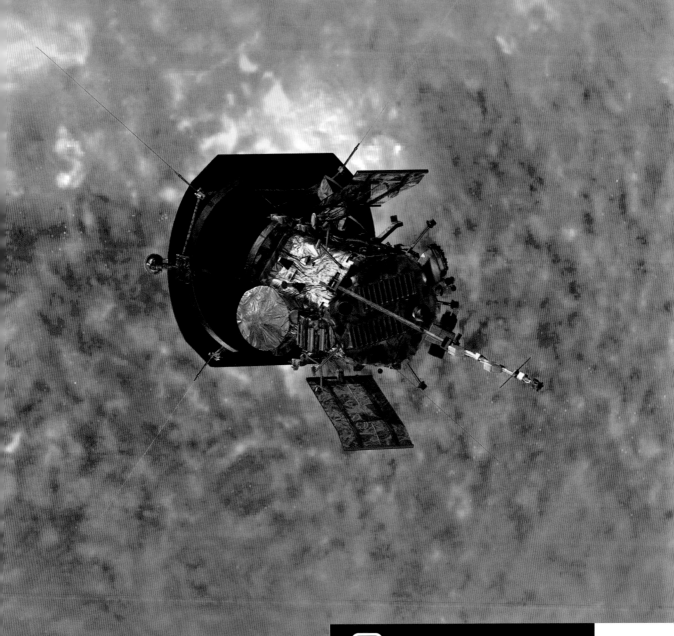

 **WATCH!**

Watch the video (see page 32).
What do you see on the Sun?

What is inside a star?

Stars are big balls of many hot gases. All stars have two gases in them – hydrogen and helium.

The star changes the hydrogen into helium and this makes the star hot.

Hydrogen changes into helium in the star's **core**.

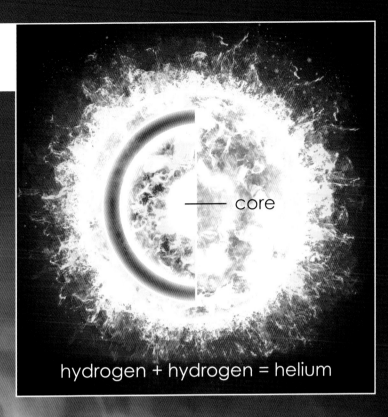

core

hydrogen + hydrogen = helium

There is helium in this balloon.

 **FIND OUT!**

Use books or the internet to find out about the Sun. How old is the Sun?

How many stars are in a galaxy?

A galaxy is a big **group** of stars and gases in space. There are billions of stars in a galaxy, and there are billions of galaxies in space!

galaxy

Our galaxy is the Milky Way.

We can see pictures when we look at the stars in the Milky Way.

 **PROJECT**

Work with a friend. Make a poster about the Milky Way. Write some facts on your poster.

19

How do we see stars?

Stars are very big. But why do they look small at night? They look small because stars are **far** from Earth. We need a **telescope** to see them well. We have very big telescopes on Earth.

mountain

Many telescopes are on mountains.

This telescope takes photos of stars at the core of the Milky Way.

THINK!

Why do you think the telescopes on Earth are so big?

Telescopes in space can see stars very well. In 1990, the Hubble Space Telescope went into space. It takes photos of everything – galaxies, nebulas, stars and planets. We know a lot about space because of Hubble.

The James Webb Space Telescope went into space in 2021. It helps us to learn about the first stars.

camera

Some space telescopes have big cameras.

▶ **WATCH!**

Watch the video (see page 32).
What happens when the spacecraft gets into space?

How far are the stars?

The Sun is the only star in our Solar System. It is 150,000,000 **kilometres** from Earth. Proxima Centauri is 40,170,000,000,000 kilometres from Earth!

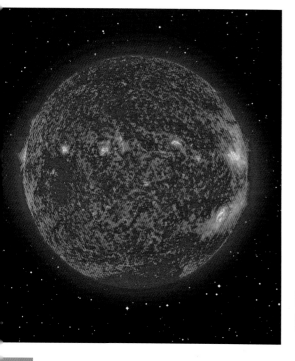

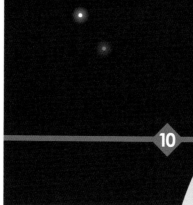

Proxima Centauri is a red-dwarf star.

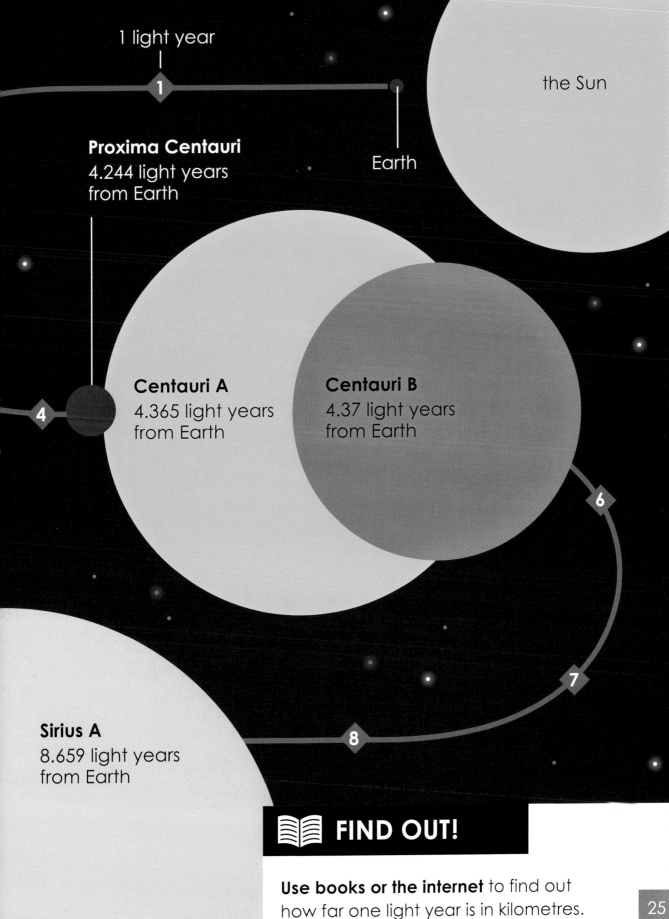

1 light year

1

the Sun

Earth

Proxima Centauri
4.244 light years
from Earth

4

Centauri A
4.365 light years
from Earth

Centauri B
4.37 light years
from Earth

6

7

Sirius A
8.659 light years
from Earth

8

📖 FIND OUT!

Use books or the internet to find out
how far one light year is in kilometres.

25

Do old stars die?

Stars live for a long time, but then they die. Stars die because they have no more hydrogen. Big stars change hydrogen into helium quickly. Their core gets very heavy and there is a supernova **explosion**.

neutron star

Supernova explosions can make neutron stars.

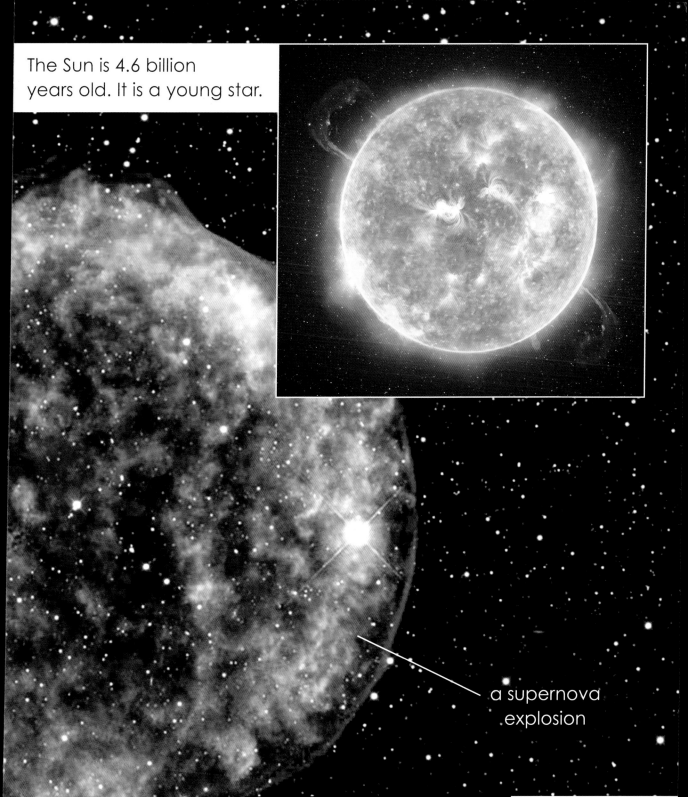

The Sun is 4.6 billion years old. It is a young star.

a supernova explosion

PROJECT

Work with a friend. Make a fact file about supernova explosions. Draw a picture to go with your fact file.

Some stars **grow** and grow before they die. They grow into red giants. Then the outside of the star **blows away**. The star's core is now a white dwarf.

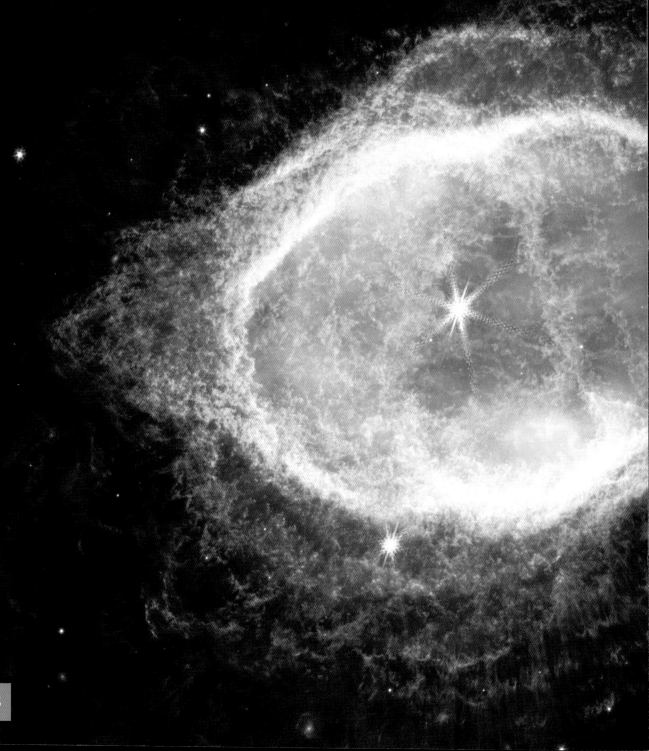

Small stars change hydrogen into helium slowly. Small stars can get very old.

Red dwarfs are very small.
They can live for 100 billion years!

 **FIND OUT!**

Use books or the internet to find
a picture of a very old star.

Quiz

Choose the correct answers.

1 A star is a . . .
   a group of planets.
   b big ball of hot gases.
   c solar system.

2 A baby star is a . . .
   a nebula.
   b protostar.
   c galaxy.

3 Very big stars are . . .
   a hypergiant stars.
   b dwarf stars.
   c yellow stars.

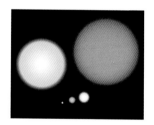

4 Blue stars are . . .
   a cold.
   b hot.
   c very, very hot.

5 Stars change . . .
  a gases into planets.
  b hydrogen into helium.
  c helium into hydrogen.

6 The Milky Way is . . .
  a a nebula.
  b a hypergiant star.
  c a galaxy.

7 We need a . . . to see stars well.
  a nebula
  b balloon
  c telescope

8 Supernova explosions can make . . .
  a neutron stars.
  b galaxies.
  c solar systems.

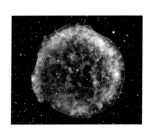

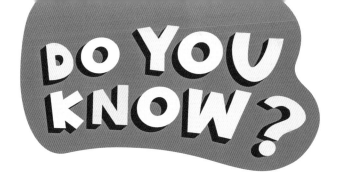

Visit www.ladybirdeducation.co.uk for
FREE DO YOU KNOW? teaching resources.

- video clips with simplified voiceover and subtitles
- video and comprehension activities
- class projects and lesson plans
- audio recording of every book
- digital version of every book
- full answer keys

To access video clips, audio tracks and digital books:

1 Go to **www.ladybirdeducation.co.uk**
2 Click 'Unlock book'
3 Enter the code below

L4Ahee5tyw

Stay safe online! Some of the DO YOU KNOW? activities ask children to do extra research online. Remember:

- ensure an adult is supervising;
- use established search engines such as Google or Kiddle;
- children should never share personal details, such as name, home or school address, telephone number or photos.

The
Met
Gala

Harper *by* Design

The Met Gala

Iconic moments of fashion from the world's most exclusive event

BALDEVA

2019
Billy Porter

If NFL fans have the Superbowl and pop tragics have Eurovision, then fashion fans have the Met Gala. For anyone interested in couture, pop culture or celebrity gossip, the first Monday in May is set aside as a day to worship the over-the-top, flamboyant, camp and often utterly bonkers creations that grace its annual red carpet.

What began as a one-off fundraiser more than 75 years ago has grown into what is now considered to be fashion's hottest (and most prohibitively expensive) ticket in town. Originally held at the Waldorf Astoria hotel in New York City in 1948, the Met Gala was created to raise funds for the Metropolitan Museum of Art's new Costume Institute. The 'Costume Institute Benefit', as it was then called, was the brainchild of influential fashion publicist and founder of New York Fashion Week, Eleanor Lambert and was a somewhat low-key affair in comparison to the pop culture phenomenon it is today.

Over the years, a veritable who's who of celebrities, socialites and notable public figures have frocked up for the Gala, including art and design heavyweights (Andy Warhol), political royalty (First Ladies Jackie Kennedy Onassis and Hillary Clinton) and real-life royalty (Princess Diana and Queen Rania of Jordan). Popstars (Cher, Madonna, Diana Ross and David Bowie), supermodels (Kate Moss, Naomi Campbell, Claudia Schiffer and Linda Evangelista), silver-screen stars (Hugh Grant, Anne Hathaway and Zendaya) and sportspeople (Serena Williams, Roger Federer and Lewis Hamilton) have also made appearances, along with – of course – fashion designers like Stella McCartney, Alexander McQueen, Yves Saint Laurent and Tom Ford, to name just a few. The Gala has always had a head for who's trending, and who has something important to say.

From the early '70s to the late '80s, *Vogue* editor Diana Vreeland steered the Met Gala through its leopard print and shoulder pad eras, before passing the torch to Anna Wintour in 1995. The long-serving editor-in-chief of *Vogue* ushered in a new, star-studded epoch for the Gala, taking it from a party for socialites to one of the most talked-about events in the world

Classic gowns have been replaced by riskier, zeitgeisty looks that delight in pushing the envelope further every year. From the outlandish to the avant-garde and the downright bizarre, Met Gala fits are all about grabbing attention and making a statement. And why not? Owning the Met Gala's red carpet is probably the best way for a celebrity to cement themselves as a style icon.

The Met Gala gives guests full licence to be as extra as they want to be, and in recent years some partygoers have gone overboard in the name of fashion – Jared Leto carrying a replica of his own head in 2019 lingers in many of our minds. So does the time an unrecognisable Doja Cat channelled Karl Lagerfeld's cat, Choupette, by purring up a storm on the red carpet in 2023. Then there are Rihanna's many iconic, viral looks that have led to Gala devotees crowning her as its unofficial queen.

The selection of quotes in this book reflects the outstanding creative spirit of the Met Gala and the guests who grace its carpets. From Diane von Fürstenberg to Timothée Chalamet, they demonstrate that self-belief, daring to be different and striving to be exceptional will always be important aspects of the Met Gala pageantry.

It is important to remember that the Met Gala is more than just an excuse for the rich and famous to parade in fantastic frocks. It is still a fundraiser responsible for raising millions of dollars for the arts. And, beyond the ostentatious displays of wealth and silly stunts, the spectacle of the Met Gala red carpet acts as an unofficial trend barometer. Just as fashion trends filter down from the runways of Paris and London, so do looks, ideas and movements from the Gala.

Fashion trends may come and go, soundbites of viral wisdom may fade with time, and a celebrity's cultural capital may rise and fall, but one thing remains certain over the years:

the Met Gala will always be in vogue.

2021
Kim Kardashian

2019
Cardi B

The 2020s

2024
Sydney Sweeney

2024
Sarah Paulson

2024
Zendaya

'DON'T TRY SO HARD TO FIT IN, *and certainly don't try so hard to be different* ... JUST TRY HARD TO BE YOU.'

Zendaya

2024
Cole Escola

2024

Gigi Hadid

2023
Bad Bunny

2023
Pedro Pascal

'IF YOUR ONLY INTENT IS TO BE SEEN, *you'll never be seen.*'

Doja Cat

2023
Doja Cat

2022
Blake Lively

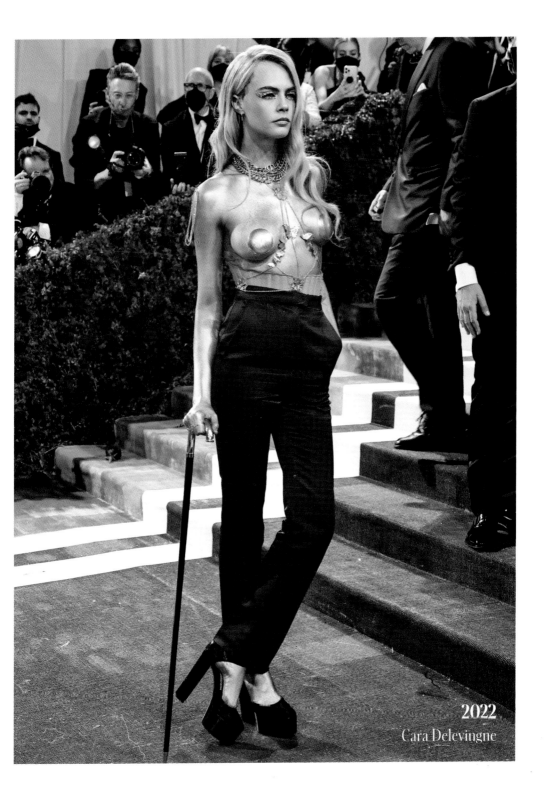

2022
Cara Delevingne

2021
Billie Eilish

2021
Timothée Chalamet

'YOU COULD BE THE CAPTAIN OF YOUR SOUL. *But you have to realise that* LIFE IS COMING FROM YOU AND NOT AT YOU, *and that takes time*.'

Timothée Chalamet

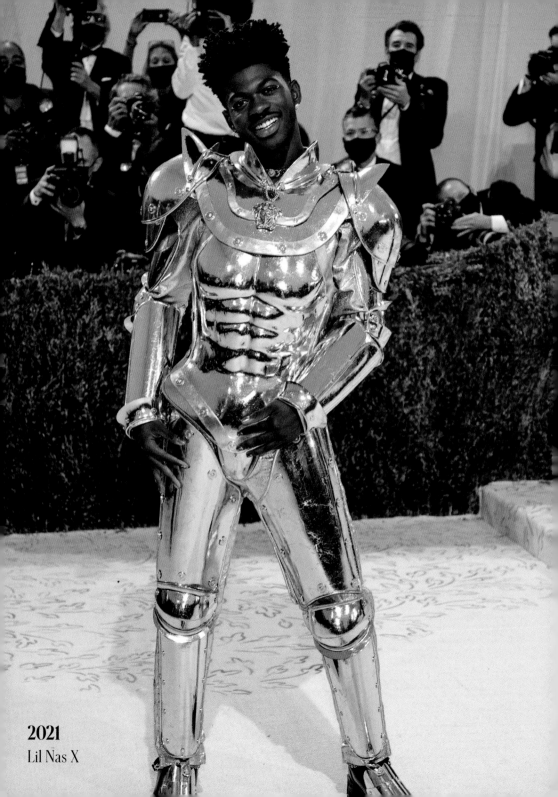

2021
Lil Nas X

2021
Alexandria Ocasio-Cortez

The
2010s

2019
Kim Kardashian

2019
Jared Leto

2019
Lady Gaga

'I LOVE MY LITTLE MONSTERS. *Now I live and create only for them.*'

Lady Gaga

2018
Ariana Grande

2018
Zendaya

2017
Katy Perry

2016
Claire Danes

2015
Beyoncé

2015
Rihanna

'I'M INTIMIDATED *by the fear of being average.*'

Taylor Swift

2014
Taylor Swift

2013
Madonna

2013
Miley Cyrus

2012
Beyoncé

'MY MOTHER
TAUGHT ME THE
IMPORTANCE
not just of being seen
BUT OF SEEING
MYSELF.'

Beyoncé

2011
André Leon Talley

2010
Christina Hendricks

The 2000s

'YOU CAN BE A PRETTY FACE, *but if you're not a nice person,* IT JUST DOESN'T WORK.'

Kate Moss

2009
Kate Moss and
Marc Jacobs

2008
David and
Victoria Beckham

2008
Katie Holmes
and Tom Cruise

2007
Lucy Liu

2007
Donatella Versace
and Hilary Swank

'THE WAY PEOPLE PERCEIVE YOU *is entirely different, often,* TO THE WAY YOU MOVE *through the world.*'

Cate Blanchett

2007
Cate Blanchett

2006
Anne Hathaway

2006
Sarah Jessica Parker

2006
va Mendes

2006
Linda Evangelista

2005
Ashley and
Mary-Kate Olsen

2004
Amber Valletta

2004
Karl Lagerfeld

'I DON'T WANT TO DO ANYTHING *over again, ever again.* I WANT ONLY TO DO *what I haven't done*.'

Karl Lagerfeld

2003
Nicole Kidman

2001
Hillary Clinton

The
1990s

1999
Whitney Houston
and Bobby Brown

1999
Gisele Bündchen

1998
Liv Tyler

1998
Claudia Schiffer

'I HAVE ALWAYS
LOVED DIFFERENCE
– *maybe because*
I was different myself,
IN SOME WAY.'

Jean Paul Gaultier

1997
Jean Paul Gaultier

1996
Linda Evangelista
and Kyle MacLachlan

1996
Diana, Princess of Wales

1995
Kate Moss

1995
Hugh Grant and
Elizabeth Hurley

1994
Anna Wintour

1993
Ralph and
Ricky Lauren

1992
Christy Turlington

1991
Joan Rivers

'I NEEDED TO SING BECAUSE NOBODY ELSE *was singing my songs.*'

David Bowie

1990
Iman, and
David Bowie

1990
Francesco Scavullo
and Naomi Campbell

'I DON'T THINK ABOUT THE WORD "FAME"... *I'm just Naomi.* AND THAT'S IT.'

Naomi Campbell

The
1980s

'I DON'T CARE FOR THE WORD "BRAND", *to be honest – it makes me feel like I'm in a* SUPERMARKET.'

Anna Wintour

1989
Anna Wintour

1989
Paloma Picasso and
Rafael Lopez Sanchez

1988
Zandra Rhodes

1987
Barbara Walters
and Merv Adelson

1986

Issey Miyake

1985
Cher

'ICON – IT'S A WORD, but I somehow don't relate to it myself.'

Cher

1984
Bob Mackie and
Bernadette Peters

1984
Diane von Fürstenberg

'WE HAVE WAY TOO MUCH DEMOCRACY IN THE CULTURE *and way too little in the society.*'

Fran Lebowitz

1983
Fran Lebowitz

1983
Linda Gray

1982
Raquel Welch

1981
Diana Ross and
Patrice Calmettes

1981
Calvin Klein
and Iman

'I READ *everything!*
I WOULD HAVE
READ THE *phone*
book IF YOU PUT
IT IN FRONT OF ME.'

Diana Vreeland

1980
Diana Vreeland

The
1970s

1979
Debbie Harry

1979
Jackie Kennedy Onassis

1979
Barbara Walters

1979
Gloria Vanderbilt

'VERY EARLY IN LIFE *I realised that the most important relationship* IS THE ONE YOU HAVE WITH YOURSELF.'

Diane von Fürstenberg

1979
Diane von Fürstenberg
and guest

1978
Egon, Prinz von Fürstenberg
and guest

1978
Valentino, and
Diana Vreeland

'I'D RATHER
DO NEW STUFF.
*New things are
always better than*
OLD THINGS.'

Andy Warhol

1977
Barbara Allen de Kwiatkowski
and Andy Warhol

1977
Halston, and
Bianca Jagger

1974
Wallis, Duchess of Windsor

1974
Cher

Harper *by* Design

An imprint of HarperCollins*Publishers*

HarperCollins*Publishers*
Australia • Brazil • Canada • France • Germany • Holland • India
Italy • Japan • Mexico • New Zealand • Poland • Spain • Sweden
Switzerland • United Kingdom • United States of America

HarperCollins acknowledges the Traditional Custodians
of the lands upon which we live and work, and pays respect
to Elders past and present.

First published on Gadigal Country in Australia in 2025
by HarperCollins*Publishers* Australia Pty Limited
ABN 36 009 913 517
harpercollins.com.au

A catalogue record for this book is available from the National Library of Australia

ISBN 978 1 4607 6735 1 (hardback)

This book is not authorized by The Metropolitan Museum of Art.

Publisher: Mark Campbell
Publishing Director: Brigitta Doyle
Senior Editor: Shannon Kelly
Cover and internal design by Mietta Yans, HarperCollins Design Studio
Copy text by Jo Stewart
Cover illustration by Sylvia Baldeva

Colour reproduction by Splitting Image Colour Studio, Wantirna, Victoria
Printed and bound in China

8 7 6 5 4 3 2 1   25 26 27 28 29